SOMETIMES RAIN WILL SHOW YOU THE LIGHT

SOMETIMES RAIN WILL
SHOW YOU THE LIGHT

A PARABLE BY A CANCER SURVIVOR

DEON L. HOGAN

XULON PRESS

Xulon Press
2301 Lucien Way #415
Maitland, FL 32751
407.339.4217
www.xulonpress.com

© 2018 by DEON L. HOGAN

Printed in the United States of America.

ISBN-13: 978-1-54564-364-8

This book is dedicated to the many men
and women who have survived cancer

In life, there's nothing like the cry of a parent who
just learned that their child or themselves has
terminal cancer. Cancer, along with its companions,
fear and denial, can cause devastation like no
other disease.

May God continue to bless the many men and
women who have not allowed cancer and its
companions to take control over their lives. Such
people who are close to me as Verlon Hogan, Jr.,
Lorence, Greylon, Karen, Paul, Cheryl, Debbie,
Ronald, Fred, Halcyon, Ronda, Linda, Larry,
Michael, Alexander, Theo, Stanley, Frank, Leonard
and many others.

ACKNOWLEDGMENTS

M any people have contributed to this book and supported me over the years. It is my privilege; therefore, to acknowledge the help I received from those who typed, edited and just made good and sound suggestions who include: Bertha, Carol, Darla, Demereal, Karen, Stephanie, Tamara, James and Warren.

FOREWORD

This work "*Sometimes Rain Will Show You the Light –
A Parable by A Cancer Survivor*" is an extremely,
dynamic from many perspectives. It is awe inspiring, spir-
itual, powerful, and provides a simple truth about what we
hold dear and the fight to remain diligent keeping hold
to a belief in greater forces at work in the universe. The
analogies among the characters and symbolism, tran-
scends the particular personal struggles Deon underwent
as a cancer survivor, but reaches the struggles of life. It
is relatable, thoughtful, and written in such a way, it could
easily be used in children's programs for at-risk-youth.

Deon's character is symbolically represented in the ten-
derness of a stranger, the sacrifice of a friend, and the
loss of something valuable. I have personally witnessed
him unselfishly serve as a federal agent, protecting the
people of Detroit and beyond. Additionally, he willingly
answered the call to serve the children of the Marshall
Alexander Youth Organization and many others through
speaking engagements.

The parables used in "*Sometimes Rain Will Show You the Light – A Parable by A Cancer Survivor*", gives the reader a sense of hope; a feeling that all is not lost and the possibility that your Mountain Lions can be defeated. I highly recommend "*Sometimes Rain Will Show You the Light – A Parable by A Cancer Survivor*" to any person, family, or group that seeks inspiration. The parables used equally apply to women, men, young, and old alike not simply those facing medical challenges but life challenges.

Cynthia D. Hayes, LSSBB, MSCIS
Executive Director
Marshall Alexander Youth Organization

PREFACE

P edro was angry because it was another hot day in the midst of a long drought with no rain in sight. He had secured his farm animals and his home while his two children were asleep, so Pedro turned in with his wife for the evening. While in bed, Pedro sensed something was wrong; something was out there. The farm animals were more restless than usual; he could hear them moving around in the barn and coop, but they were not making any of their usual night sounds. Neither could Pedro hear any crickets chirping, frogs croaking, or the occasional hoot of an owl. There was an unusual quietness about the place.

Pedro got out of bed and looked out the window, only to see a blanket of fog coming down the mountains. He watched as the fog blanketed the trees, the roads, and eventually his home. As Pedro stood there thinking how eerie this fog was, he realized that he could no longer see any farther than his front porch. When he returned to bed, his wife, Maria, inquired about the quietness of the animals. She stated that she felt something was wrong. Pedro shared with her that he just saw a blanket of fog coming down the mountains and over their home. She replied that fog in a drought such as this is highly unusual, given the dry conditions. Pedro then told his wife that he hadn't seen any wild animals such as rabbits, deer, beavers, or any of the wildlife that usually visited the farm at night. Maria stated that the wildlife may have moved on to find water. Maria expressed concern about the farm, and Pedro held her tight as they fell off to sleep.

Later that night, Pedro was awakened by his two children running into the bedroom, frightened by the roar of a mountain lion. Pedro grabbed his rifle and a lantern and headed out the door. The fog was so dense that the lantern light reflected back toward Pedro, rendering him blind. Pedro could hear the chickens squawking, the cows and the sheep bellowing, the crumpling of the chicken coop, and the barn door being ripped off its hinges.

Pedro heard the loud snarling, growling, and squealing of an animal being attacked. Overwhelmed with fear, Pedro retreated and returned home to protect his family from the vicious predator. In the morning, Pedro reluctantly made his way to the barn to assess the damage which had been done the night before. As the fog lifted, what he saw was total devastation. The chicken coop was seriously damaged with dead chickens lying on the ground.

The barn door had been torn from its hinges and scratch marks from the mountain lion could be seen from where he stood. As Pedro entered the barn, he observed his oldest and dearest cow lying dead. All his sheep and the rest of the cows had fled. As Pedro's emotions began to swell within him, he promised himself and God that he would hunt that beast over all creation and kill it. "That beast has terrorized my home for the last time. I'll find a way to get you, you evil devil!"

As Pedro was leaving the barn with tears in his eyes, he saw his old friend Miguel, one of the villagers, approaching on horseback. Miguel, seeing the condition that Pedro's farm was in, realized that the mountain lion had been there. Still mounted on his horse, Miguel expressed sorrow to Pedro regarding the attack on his farm. He then told Pedro of an attack in the village approximately five miles away. According to Miguel, the mountain lion came into the village and attacked one of the children as the child lay in bed. Miguel stated that he and about eleven other villagers were going up in the mountains to hunt the beast. Miguel then suggested that Pedro join the hunting party to help hunt and kill this vicious animal. As vigilant as Pedro felt, he instinctively knew that it would be best for him to remain close to his home and the village in case that devil returned. Pedro told Miguel that if he and the villagers did not get that beast, he had made a commitment to God that he would find and slay the beast.

Weeks had gone by before Pedro learned that only three villagers had returned, with Miguel being one. Pedro decided to go and visit his friend Miguel at his home in the village. Miguel's wife, Rita, met Pedro at the door and in a low voice said, "Pedro, the mountain lion attacked Miguel, and his injuries are critical. Miguel may not make it!" Rita then escorted Pedro to the bedroom; he saw his friend Miguel lying in bed but wasn't prepared for severity of the damage the mountain lion had caused. Miguel had bandages around his head and throat, and a gaping hole in his left thigh. The beast had severed Miguel's right arm. Pedro was moved to tears when he thought of how Miguel had just left him two weeks ago, a healthy yet angry man determined to catch the mountain lion. Pedro thought to himself, *"It was only by God's grace that Miguel is still alive."*

Pedro sat in a chair at Miguel's bedside, and he gently placed his hand on his shoulder. Breaking the intense moment of silence, Pedro inquired as to what happened in the mountains. Miguel, in a whispering voice barely audible, explained that they tracked the mountain lion for two weeks. They saw that animal entering into a thick area of trees. They set traps to capture the beast, but the beast was able to take the bait without being cap-tured. It was clearly apparent that they were on the moun-tain lion's terrain. One by one, with lightning speed and quickness, the mountain lion started stalking and killing villagers. Attacks came from everywhere all through the night. They shot at the beast, but because it was so agile and cunning, they missed. The beast would double back, come up from out of the trees, and attack them without warning. In the end, nine villagers were lost to that mountain lion. As the three of them were returning home, the predator ambushed them once again. As Miguel was sitting upon his horse, the mountain lion jumped out of the bushes, frightening the horse, who threw Miguel onto the ground. That mountain lion, according to Miguel, appeared to have weighed three hundred pounds and was on Miguel so quick that he was unable to defend himself. It grabbed Miguel by the head with its mighty teeth and sliced at Miguel's throat with its claws. Miguel was able to shake loose from the beast, and that was when the mountain lion grabbed his arm, severing it from his body. Miguel tried to crawl away and was bitten on his thigh. Fearing death and weak from loss of blood, Miguel said he began praying to God, when suddenly he heard a gunshot. The beast released Miguel and ran back into the woods. The two other villagers saved Miguel's life and got him home safely. With a stronger voice, Miguel shouted, "Pedro, be careful! The mountain lion is huge, cunning, and a killer! That beast still lives."

"SOMETIMES RAIN WILL SHOW YOU THE LIGHT"

A Parable by a Cancer Survivor

Ringo, a cowboy traveling down an old dusty road through a small village in Mexico, came across Pedro, who was training a puppy. Ringo thought to himself that this had to be one of the prettiest pups he had ever seen. Ringo introduced himself to Pedro and said he thought that the puppy had beautiful markings. Ringo explained that he trained dogs for traveling rodeos. He believed Pedro's puppy would be ideal for the rodeos. Ringo offered Pedro twenty-five thousand pesos to purchase the pup.

"Gracias Señor, but the puppy is not for sale," Pedro replied. "I am training this pup to save my village."

Ringo raised his offer. "I will give you 50,000 pesos. I want this puppy."

"No, Señor, no amount of money for this pup. You must understand that we have a mountain lion in this area that hunts and kills our livestock. I am up early every morning to come out to train this pup. We start faithfully at six in the morning, and we train until sunset. I have neglected my fields, the water in the stream has run dry because the dam is broken, and the chickens are running all over the place because the chicken coop is damaged. The cows and the sheep are out in the forest because the barn door was torn off its hinges. My children are afraid to come outside, my wife is threatening to leave me, and the drought that we are in has left my corn fields bare. Still, I train this pup to save my village and my home."

Ringo asked, how is training this puppy going to help you?"

"You see, the mountain lion comes out of the mountains and terrorized the village by attacking a child while asleep in his bed. That same mountain lion attacked my home, killing my prized cow, sheep, and several chickens! I promised God, myself, and the villagers that I would kill this beast. This devil of an animal has made our home and village his hunting ground. The children in the village and my children are scared to come out after dark because of the mountain lion. We have tried for months to hunt this mountain lion down, but he is devious, smart, and unpredictable. Until now, we have had no way of catching that devil of an animal.

"Señor Ringo, one day after an attack, I mounted my house in search of my livestock. As I traveled along this dusty road, I came across a female dog lying in the grass. There was no doubt that she had encountered that devil. Even in the state that I found her, I could tell that she once was a beautiful dog. She had been mauled, and parts of her were missing, eaten by that beast! Worst yet, I could see that she was full of puppies, all of them dead from the attack, except one!"

Ringo said, "Let me guess, this puppy, right?"

"Sí Señor, somehow he had found his way out and was crawling around his dead mother. His eyes were not open yet, but he was able to feel her presence. Seeing this puppy and the condition of his mother and litter mates, I took the puppy in my arms and thanked God for the answers to my prayers to catch that mountain lion. I named him 'Milagro' or 'Miracle.' Señor Ringo, the way I see it, Miracle and I both have the same need to catch this mountain lion."

Ringo said that he was going up the road and would return in a year to see if Pedro would be willing to sell at that time. Pedro replied, "Señor, you can return all you want, but I am not selling Miracle. He will save my village."

Months went by, and every day like clockwork, Pedro would train Miracle. During Miracle's training, Pedro would take the hair from the mountain lion he found in the barn after an attack on his animals and use it as a training tool. As part of Miracle's training, Pedro would hide the hair in various places for Miracle to find. Pedro tied the hair into a ball and placed it in pail of water. Miracle was able to submerge his mouth into the pail of water and retrieve the hair ball. Pedro would also hide the hair deep in the base of a hollow tree where Miracle could submerge his body so deep into the tree that Pedro could only see his tail. A short time later, Miracle would emerge from the hole with the ball of hair in his teeth. Pedro would hide the hair high in the tree, where Miracle was unable to reach, but would stand at the base of the tree and bark. To build Miracle's endurance, Pedro would tie the hair to the tail of a horse and run for miles into the mountain with Miracle trailing behind. No matter where Pedro would hide the ball of the mountain lion's hair, Miracle was able to hunt it and retrieve it. Every time Miracle found the mountain lion's hair, Pedro would reward Miracle with hugs and words of praise, such as, "That a boy, good dog," while feeding him small bits of beef jerky. Miracle grew into a beautiful dog, and his hunting skills were impeccable.

One night after training Miracle, Pedro returned to his home and found that Maria and the children were no longer there. Pedro, feeling the void, came to the realization that he had forsaken his family. Overwhelmed with sorrow and with tears in his eyes, Pedro called out, "Maria," and then said, "I am so sorry, but I will kill this beast and make our house a safe home again. I promise."

Pedro cried himself to sleep, and while sleeping, he heard the loud roar of a mountain lion and Miracle barking. He rushed to the window and saw Miracle break loose and run into the forest and up the mountain. Pedro grabbed his rifle, a lantern, a lunch box he had prepared, and a canteen filled with water. He could hear Miracle barking in the near distance, but he could not catch him.

On the second day, Pedro continued to hunt for Miracle and the mountain lion. But Miracle's bark was becoming more and more faint.

On the third day, Miracle was even farther away, steadily climbing higher and higher into the mountains. During the daylight, Pedro could see the mountain lion's paw prints, followed by Miracle's prints. Miracle was hot on the mountain lion's trail; however, he was still too far ahead for Pedro to see.

On the fourth day, Pedro seemed to be getting a little closer, but he noticed that his supplies were beginning to run short. The oil in the lantern began to run low; therefore, he could barely see at night. His water supply was about one-third filled, and his food supply was gone. His horse had been without water for the past three days, yet Pedro pressed on to find his Miracle and to kill the Mountain lion.

On the fifth day, the lantern burned out completely, and Pedro could no longer travel by night. Yet, he could still hear Miracle pressing further and further ahead. Determined not to let his prized possession die, Pedro continued to go forward up the mountain.

On the sixth day, Pedro found himself completely out of water, with no food, no lantern, and his horse weak from lack of water, but he still pressed on.

On the seventh day, Pedro could no longer hear Miracle barking and began to worry. Pedro began to pray. "Please God, don't let anything happen to Miracle." He then called out to Miracle, but there was no response. Pedro called again, "Miracle!" and prayed, "Please God, take care of my Miracle. All the time that I put into training and working with him, don't let it be in vain. Don't forsake me, God! Let my Miracle be alive!" Pedro shouted again, "Miracle!" Still no response, but Pedro was able to find the tracks of the mountain lion with Miracle following in the same direction. As Pedro reached the clearing of the mountain top, he saw a figure lying in the grass. Pedro said, "No, no! Don't let it be Miracle!"

"All my training, the loss of my wife and children, the death of my prized cow, and the terrorizing of my village. God don't forsake me—not now, not with Miracle! Let that be the beast that I am so faithfully hunting. Oh God spare me the pain of yet another loss, not my Miracle!" As he got closer and closer, he realized the figure was Miracle, half eaten and mauled by the mountain lion. Pedro fell to his knees as tears uncontrollably came from his face, and he said, over and over again, "No God, no God, not this, not my Miracle!" As Pedro was on his knees next to Miracle, he recalled the first time he saw Miracle lying next to his mother. Pedro thought to himself, *I've had enough of this beast. With all my might and with all my faith in God, I will destroy that Mountain lion.*

Pedro cried as he thought about the good times that he and Miracle had shared—all the hunting exercises that started early morning and lasted late into the night. After all that training, that devil of a mountain lion had done the same to Miracle as he had Miracle's mother. After burying Miracle, weary, cold, thirsty, hungry, and with no light, Pedro prayed to God for help. Totally exhausted and emotionally drained, he fell asleep, only to be awakened a few hours later by a drop of rain. The raindrop turned into a sprinkle, the sprinkles turned into a shower, and Pedro looked to the heavens and thanked God.

The water was enough to fill his canteen and provide for his horse. The shower turned into a full-fledged thunderstorm with howling winds and virtual downpours of rain. It rained so hard that a stream formed and began to flow down the mountain. Pedro, seeing this, realized he was lost no longer. He was familiar with the stream that ran from the mountain down to the river and valley that led to the stream that ran past his house, so ideally, if he followed the stream, he would find his way home.

Determined to find his way home, Pedro began to follow the stream down the mountain, praying as he went, telling God that as faithfully as he worked to train Miracle, he would begin to work to praise His name. Pedro felt incomplete and remorseful that he had lost his prized possession without killing the mountain lion. As he followed the stream, he noticed that it curved around a mountain ledge. When he began to cross under the mountain ledge, he noticed a pair of soul-piercing eyes. These eyes appeared to be hollow, the cold yet fiery, burning eyes of a mountain lion looking down on him.

"Finally, we meet!" Pedro said to the mountain lion. "Come on, you beast! I've been waiting on this moment, for all that you have taken from me. I will send you back to hell from which you came!"

Pedro reached for his rifle, but because it was wet, it slipped from his hands and tumbled down the mountain. Now, looking at certain death, face to face with the Mountain lion about to pounce on him, Pedro said, "Come on, I'll take you on with my bare hands!"

He pulled out a knife and began to pray. "Oh God, give me the strength to kill this beast! Help me, Lord!" As the wind began to pick up, there was a terrible, loud crack in the air. As Pedro began to retreat, he saw a large shadow falling toward him. A giant oak tree fell upon the mountain lion, killing him as he stood ready to pounce.

"God you have not forsaken me!" Pedro shouted with elation. "Your mighty hand has killed the beast." Pedro was overcome with emotion, laughter, and tears of joy. "Glory to God," he said.

Still shaking and trembling with fear and excitement, he climbed up on his horse's back to pull himself up onto the mountain ledge. After seeing the mountain lion lying there helpless, Pedro realized how small that mountain lion was. It's amazing how fear and denial can make something seem so insurmountable. As he struggled to get the mountain lion from under the tree and off the mountain ledge, Pedro kicked and punched the dead beast, crying uncontrollably. "For all that you have taken from me, I take it back, in your death!" Pedro lowered himself and the mountain lion from the ledge, then tied the mountain lion to the back of his horse and started his journey down the mountain.

As he traveled, following the stream, he realized that the mountain terrain had changed. Parts of it had been washed away by the heavy rain. Pedro altered his route to avoid ditches and craters the waters were creating. The road was slippery, the horse stumbled and fell, but Pedro held on and continued his path down to the river. Once he reached the river, he knew he was safe, so he followed the river down to the stream that led to his home. From the horizon, Pedro could see the glow of his small village. As he approached his home, he could see a light coming from his kitchen window.

The closer he got to his farm, the more he could not believe what had transpired. The chickens were in the damaged chicken coop hiding from the rain, the sheep and cows were in the barn seeking shelter, the beavers had built a dam in the stream, the water had begun to fill the reservoir, and his cornfields had begun to sprout from the rain. Just as he and his horse arrived, the door flew open, and his two children ran out shouting, "Papi, we have been looking for you for six days. Mommy is in the house. She's been crying, waiting for you." Finally, the rain stopped.

Several weeks passed, and Ringo, as promised, came back down the road. He encountered Pedro sitting on the side of the road with a basket of corn. "Wow! This place has changed a great deal in a year." Ringo said. "It looks very nice, and where is Milagro—or Miracle?"

Pedro replied, "Sí Señor, the place has changed a great deal. As you can see, Miracle is no longer here, but the mountain lion's skin hangs on my door.

"What happened to Miracle?" Ringo asked.

Pedro replied, "It started with an attack on my village, where a young child was asleep in his home and attacked by a mountain lion. That same night, that beast attacked my home, killing several of my animals. The child survived the attack, and several men from the village, including my friend Miguel, went hunting for that beast. During the hunt, the mountain lion killed several villagers and mortally wounded my friend Miguel. Miguel survived long enough to make it home and told the story of how the mountain lion ambushed him and the villagers.

"As you know, I raised Miracle to help me take revenge on the mountain lion. During the months of training, I neglected my farm and my family, which lead to my wife and children leaving me. One night, Señor, as I slept, the mountain lion came down and attacked my house.

Miracle broke loose and chased the mountain lion up the mountain. I followed Miracle for seven days. During that period of time, I ran out of food and water, and I had no light. By the time I reached Miracle, the mountain lion had killed him. After burying Miracle, I was tired, emotionally drained, and lost. I did only what a man could do—I prayed to God. He gave me an answer in the form of rain. You never know how or when God is going to answer your prayers, but if you believe in God, your prayers will be answered. It rained enough for me to fill my canteen, and the rain developed a stream for me to follow home.

"As I was following the stream that passed under a mountain ledge, I came face to face with the mountain lion. I was so tired and fed up with the mountain lion by that time, that I did not care whether I lived or died. It was either him or me. I pulled out my rifle, but it fell down the mountain. When I was face to face with that beast, I challenged him to come on, as I pulled my knife out, ready to fight him, man to beast. He was about to pounce on me when a great wind came and pushed over an oak tree, killing the mountain lion. I was so hurt and angry when pulling that mountain lion from under the tree, that I punched and kicked the dead beast. After several minutes of emotional outburst, I was finally able to remove the carcass. I dragged that beast to the edge of the mountain ledge and secured it to the back of my horse.

"As I followed that stream down the mountain, the road was not easy. When I got home, I was elated to find the chickens in the damaged chicken coop and my reservoir filled with water from the beavers who built the dam. Also, the cows and the sheep were in the barn seeking shelter. I noticed corn sprouting in the cornfields, and best of all, my wife and children were home. GLORY BE TO GOD! GLORY BE TO GOD!

"Every day, I praise His name just as faithfully as I trained Miracle. I give my total survival and my life to God Almighty, and I realize now that Miracle was just a tool, just as I am."

EPILOGUE

D eep in the base of an old hollow oak tree amongst the ledge of a mountain lie four teenage mountain lion cubs. The water from the rain begins to fill the den in which the mountain lions are living. One by one, the cubs begin to emerge with the alpha male staking out his territory in the southern mountain regions of Mexico. Each of the remaining mountain lion cubs emerge, taking different directions, north, east, and west, as they began their own lives, covering miles and miles of territory.

PARABLE

As you read this story, you can make parallels to your own life as to how God has worked miracles and touched you in some way.

As for me, after years of therapy, I realized that I was Pedro, and Pedro was me! I created that mountain lion forged from the hurt and pain that engulfed me during my childhood. While I was growing up and living with an alcoholic father, our household situation was less than ideal. I silently endured the pain.

As a pre-teen, running away from the hurt and pain I endured in my home life, I eventually joined a gang. This led to an incident in which I was accused of causing an injury to a rival gang member, landing me in the juvenile court system. This was followed by a series of traumatic events that transpired in my life. My father was in a serious vehicle accident that left him disfigured. Shortly after that, he was burned during a fire in my childhood home, where we lost everything. My father survived both; however, my brother committed suicide at a young age as he dealt with his own issues. As a teen, I also watched my best friend, Larry, die on the football field in high school.

As black men, we are raised to endure pain in silence and not to express difficult emotions outwardly. I held onto hatred from deep within my soul. I ran from pain by indulging myself in whatever endeavors I decided in life. As an adult, like Pedro, I engaged in so many activities outside my home that led to my divorce and my wife and daughter moving to another state.

I gave life to the beast by not dealing with the hurt and pain from my childhood that had been building up inside of me for years. I ran, literally, in track and field from high school through college, never confronting or dealing with the issues of my youth, and like Pedro, I faithfully worked and was subconsciously running away from myself.

Miracle represented a job with the US Government, where I was detailed on serious and dangerous missions, often taking me away from my family for months at a time. These details involved guarding US presidential candidates during a campaign season. While detailed with the Secret Service, it was my duty to secure venues ahead of the presidential candidate's arrival. This would be done by participating in a twenty-one-day jump team. The jump team consisted of agents from various governmental agencies that would travel to twenty-one different cities ahead of the presidential candidate, securing venues before the candidate's arrival. I would work for twenty-one days, then was off for two weeks, where I would return back to my regular duties until I was back on the campaign trail.

I was also detailed to Los Angeles, California for six months during the civil unrest that occurred after the Rodney King verdict in the early 1990s. During that time, it was our duty to retrieve firearms that were stolen during the riots. Later, I was detailed for sixty days to investigate the burning of black churches in Mississippi and Alabama, during which time several churches were burned, making national news. Of all the details, I was most apprehensive about the Beltway Sniper detail, where I spent forty-five days on a law enforcement task force investigating random shootings in the Washington, DC area. During this investigation, the atmosphere was contentious because gunshots were coming from unknown locations. We were very relieved the perpetrators were captured.

On the weekends when I wasn't working for the agency, my oldest brother and I would work as landscapers, beginning work at six a.m. and concluding our day by nine p.m. On Saturdays, I would stop, pick up my daughter for breakfast, and after breakfast, I would return to my landscaping job. On Sundays, I would attend early morning church service, and after church, my brother and I would return to landscaping, where I specialized in flower beds and maintaining lawns.

On the days when I wasn't working with the federal government, I worked as a personal trainer and would train college-bound students in what I call "transitional sports training." During this training, I would introduce young men and women to various running techniques that would help them transition from high school to college. In doing this, I would also counsel and mentor them in how to respect themselves and others as they headed off to college.

As a massage therapist, on Tuesdays and Thursdays I serviced a group of ten women stricken with multiple sclerosis. During these massage therapy sessions, I would concentrate on flexibility and strengthening. I would do up to four or five massages after completing a full day of work at the agency.

During the holiday season, my catering business flourished. I was hired to cook or bake dishes, including cheesecakes. My cheesecakes became so popular that during one Christmas season, I had thirty orders, which took a week to complete. I received cheesecake orders from coast to coast. All of these things took time away from the people I love and who love me.

The mountain lion in this story represents the lung cancer that I was blessed to find at an early stage. Just like cancer, the mountain lion is highly adaptable and very dangerous, with tremendous leaping ability. It is also known by many names, such as puma, panther, and catamount. Cancer also comes in many forms and is called many things, such as Leukemia,

Carcinoma, and Melanoma, among other names. Cancer also has tremendous leaping abilities, often referred to as metastasizing. In the story, as the mountain lion, or cancer, was about to pounce on me, God struck it down—not with an oak tree, but with doctors and medication.

As I recovered from this cancer, the road that I took up to the mountain was not the same road that I am taking now. There have been many changes in my life as I try to find my way back home. No longer do I want or need to work long hours on the job. My desire to work outside my home has been diminished, and just like Pedro, I promise to faithfully praise God's name and give my testimony to all who want to listen.

Upon my return to work, I was greeted by a number of people who had prayed for me and showered me with well wishes and "welcome backs." To those people, I would like to give my sincere thanks. To all my family and friends, who found me to be more of a challenge than usual and difficult to be around at times, but were very patient and understanding with me, I would like to take the time to say thanks to each and every one of you. May God continue to bless you in every way.

Love, Deon.

ABOUT THE AUTHOR

D eon was born the fourth of five children on the lower east side of Detroit, Michigan to Verlon and Annie Hogan. He gave his life to Christ at an early age and was baptized at a local church. During his childhood, Deon was always known as one of the swiftest kids in the neighborhood when it came to running. Upon entering high school, at the direction of his best friend Larry Smith, Deon excelled in both football and track. During a tackling drill at Kettering High School, Larry was tackled and died on the field of a brain aneurysm. The football team dedicated its season to Larry and went on to win the city championship. Deon dedicated his track career to Larry and went undefeated, winning the city track meet on three different occasions, setting the city record in the 400 meter. He further excelled in the state track meet, where he also set the state record in the 400 meter and 880 relays. During his senior year, he won the 100 and 200 meter.

Deon later received a track scholarship to the University of Kansas. At the University of Kansas, Deon excelled in sprints and, in his freshman year, won four events in the conference championship and was named MVP of the meet. The following year, at an indoor conference track meet, Deon established a new world record in the 400 meter and was again named MVP of the conference track meet. In his senior year at the University of Kansas, Deon broke his own world record in the 400 meter. Overall, in his track career, Deon achieved All-American six times, all Big Eight Conference sixteen times, two world records, two MVPs, was named captain three times, and set four school records.

After graduating from the University of Kansas, Deon began his career as a special agent with the federal government, where he participated and investigated such notable events as the Los Angeles riots, the Washington DC sniper, and the 1996 Olympic Games. He guarded Presidents Ronald Reagan, George H.W. Bush, Bill Clinton, and George W. Bush. He also provided protection for Vice Presidents Dan Quayle and Dick Cheney. While working detail at the state department, he provided protection detail for the Presidents of Estonia and Sudan.

During that time, Deon was married, and from that union, he had one child named Dionna. While working out, Deon hit his sternum with a barbell, and a calcium deposit began to grow. He pursued medical attention, and after several months of testing consisting of x-rays, MRIs, and CT scans, it was determined that the calcium deposit was just a calcium deposit, but a spot was noted on his right lung. In 2007, Deon was diagnosed with stage one lung cancer and underwent surgery to remove his right bottom lobe. During his recovery, Deon had a sleepless night and began to write *Sometimes Rain Will Show You the Light: A Parable for a Cancer Survivor.*

Deon is now retired and in good health, enjoying time with his daughter, grandchildren, friends, and extended family.

CPSIA information can be obtained
at www.ICGtesting.com
Printed in the USA
BVHW09s1114011018
528932BV00033B/2866/P